Have a big idea?
Ready to make It happen?

LET'S GET STARTED!

This 10-step workbook will guide you through the process of taking your idea and turning it into a business.

Make sure to take breaks to doodle, write, and grow your idea. The more you let your mind wander and explore, the more your idea will grow into something great!

 Keep a lookout for tips, ideas and inspiration along the way.

1

THE BIG IDEA

What kind of business will it be? What gave you the idea? What excites you about it?

....

....

....

....

....

....

....

....

....

....

Have lots of different ideas? That's ok! List them all; then choose the one that you know the most about and have the best skills or resources to make happen.

DOODLE BREAK!

Doodle, draw or write some more!

2

WHAT IT SOLVES

Every good idea starts with a problem that needs solving or an opportunity to improve upon something.

What problem does your business solve or improve on?

....

....

....

....

....

....

....

....

 Businesses that solve a specific problem are the most successful. Try to hone in on one main idea that everything your business does helps to solve or improve.

DOODLE BREAK!

Doodle, draw or write some more!

WHY IT MATTERS

Who can your idea help and how can it help make the world a better place?

....
....
....
....
....
....
....
....
....
....

 If you were to donate a portion of your sales to a charity, what charity would be close to your heart or relate to the work you'll do with your business?

DOODLE BREAK!

Doodle, draw or write some more!

WHO IS YOUR CUSTOMER?

Think about what kind of person would be interested in your business.

Is it kids? Moms? Soccer players? Math lovers? Write down all the kinds of people you think would be interested and why.

WHO	WHY
....	....
....	....
....	....
....	....
....	....
....	....
....	....

Think about all the different ways your business could meet people's needs. and what they have in common., how they are different.

DOODLE BREAK!

Doodle, draw or write some more!

5

DO THE RESEARCH

There's always lots to learn, especially when starting something new.

Google similar businesses and write down what would you do the same, differently, who you think their customer is and anything else that stands out.

....
....
....
....
....
....

Worried there's another business doing the same idea you had? Don't worry! How many different grocery stores or shoe stores are there out there? People like options - just focus on what makes your idea special or unique.

5

DO THE RESEARCH

Need more space? Keep the Ideas flowing!

....
....
....
....
....
....
....
....
....
....
....

Make sure to write down what other companies are charging and how they talk about their business. You'll want to reference back to this information later on!

DOODLE BREAK!

Doodle, draw or write some more!

6

CHOOSE A NAME

Now the fun stuff! What do you want to name your business?

A good business name should describe what your business offers, be easy to pronounce and unique to your idea. List out all the ideas you have and see if one stands out as your favorite.

....

....

....

....

....

....

....

 Share your ideas with your family and friends and ask what they think and what Ideas they have. The more input you get the better before making a decision.

CHOOSE A NAME

Need more space? Keep the ideas flowing!

DOODLE BREAK!

Doodle, draw or write some more!

GET YOURSELF ORGANIZED

Making lists is a great way to get organized.

What supplies will you need?

....

....

....

....

....

....

....

....

....

 Think about all the things you will need to run your business. For example if you're baking, making lemonade or making slime, what ingredients will you need to buy?

GET YOURSELF ORGANIZED

Create some more lists of your own.

....
....
....
....
....
....
....
....
....
....
....
....
....

DOODLE BREAK!

Doodle, draw or write some more!

PLAN YOUR COSTS

Time for more lists!
What costs will your business require?

::	::::::::
::	::::::::
::	::::::::
::	::::::::
::	::::::::
::	::::::::
::	::::::::
::	::::::::
::	::::::::
::	::::::::

Not sure where to start? Next time you're at the store, check the prices of the items you think you'll need, or ask your parent for advise.

DOODLE BREAK!

Doodle, draw or write some more!

9

PLAN YOUR PRICES

Have you thought about what you will charge for your product or service?

Go back to the research you did see what others are charging, and make sure you're charging more than your costs.

....
....
....
....
....
....
....

 Not sure where to start? Estimate how many customers you think you can get in the first month and how much you think each will spend. Then make sure the supply costs for the month are lower than your projected sales.

DOODLE BREAK!

Doodle, draw or write some more!

10

GET ONLINE

A good next step now that you've gotten organized is to set up a website so you can tell people where they can learn more about your business.

Things you'll need to create a website:

- [ ] A computer with Internet access

- [ ] A content outline. This includes a list of all the pages your website will have and what the main topics will be for each page. Look back at the websites you checked out in your research phase for ideas. It's ok to steal some ideas as long as you say and do it all in your own way.

- [ ] Will you be creating videos to launch your business? Make a list of these too, along with an outline of what you want each video to talk about.

 There are lots of options to start a free website, or ask a grown-up to help you get signed up for a paid account. Just make sure to add it to your cost sheet!

10

GET ONLINE

Have any lists you need to make for your content or video plans?

....

....

....

....

....

....

....

....

....

....

 This should Include why your business matters, why people should care about your business, and how they can contact you, buy.order or sign up.

GET ONLINE

Writing your website content.

What's the first thing you want people to know when they come to your website? Keep it short and to the point!

....

....

....

....

....

....

....

....

....

 This should Include why your business matters, why people should care about your business, and how they can contact you, buy.order or sign up.

LAUNCH THAT WEBSITE AND TELL EVERYONE YOU KNOW ABOUT IT!

CELEBRATE!

If you made it this far and your business is up and running, congratulations my friend! That's a huge accomplishment - you should be proud of yourself!

www.ingramcontent.com/pod-product-compliance
Lightning Source LLC
Chambersburg PA
CBHW051942210526
45473CB00006B/2349